STARVING THE STRESS GREMLIN

by the same author

Starving the Anger Gremlin
A Cognitive Behavioural Therapy Workbook on Anger Management for Young People
Kate Collins-Donnelly
ISBN 978 1 84905 286 3
eISBN 978 0 85700 621 9

Starving the Anxiety Gremlin
A Cognitive Behavioural Therapy Workbook on Anxiety Management for Young People
Kate Collins-Donnelly
ISBN 978 1 84905 341 9
eISBN 978 0 85700 673 8

of related interest

The Panicosaurus
Managing Anxiety in Children Including Those with Asperger Syndrome
K.I. Al-Ghani
Illustrated by Haitham Al-Ghani
ISBN 978 1 84905 356 3
eISBN 978 0 85700 706 3

Helping Children to Cope with Change, Stress and Anxiety
A Photocopiable Activities Book
Deborah M. Plummer
Illustrated by Alice Harper
ISBN 978 1 84310 960 0
eISBN 978 0 85700 366 9

Focusing and Calming Games for Children
Mindfulness Strategies and Activities to Help Children to Relax, Concentrate and Take Control
Deborah M. Plummer
Illustrated by Jane Serrurier
ISBN 978 1 84905 143 9
eISBN 978 0 85700 344 7

What Children Need to be Happy, Confident and Successful
Step by Step Positive Psychology to Help Children Flourish
Jeni Hooper
ISBN 978 1 84905 239 9
eISBN 978 0 85700 483 3

Frog's Breathtaking Speech
How Children (and Frogs) Can Use the Breath to Deal with Anxiety, Anger and Tension
Michael Chissick
Illustrated by Sarah Peacock
ISBN 978 1 84819 091 7
eISBN 978 0 85701 074 2

STARVING THE STRESS GREMLIN

A COGNITIVE BEHAVIOURAL THERAPY WORKBOOK ON STRESS MANAGEMENT FOR YOUNG PEOPLE

Kate Collins-Donnelly

Jessica Kingsley *Publishers*
London and Philadelphia

First published in 2013
by Jessica Kingsley Publishers
73 Collier Street
London N1 9BE, UK
and
400 Market Street, Suite 400
Philadelphia, PA 19106, USA

www.jkp.com

Library of Congress Cataloging in Publication Data
A CIP catalog record for this book is available from the Library of Congress

British Library Cataloguing in Publication Data
A CIP catalogue record for this book is available from the British Library

ISBN 978 1 84905 340 2
eISBN 978 0 85700 672 1

Printed and bound by CPI Group (UK) Ltd, Croydon CR0 4YY

MIX
Paper from
responsible sources
FSC
www.fsc.org
FSC® C013604

Contents

ACKNOWLEDGEMENTS 6

ABOUT THE AUTHOR 7

INFORMATION FOR PARENTS AND PROFESSIONALS 9

INTRODUCTION 13

1. WHAT IS STRESS? 17
2. YOU'RE NOT ON YOUR OWN: STRESS IN OTHER PEOPLE 25
3. MY STRESS 29
4. THE STRESS GREMLIN: HOW STRESS OCCURS 39
5. EFFECTS OF STRESS 53
6. STARVING THE STRESS GREMLIN: AN INTRODUCTION TO STRESS MANAGEMENT 61
7. STARVING THE STRESS GREMLIN: MANAGING YOUR THOUGHTS 65
8. STARVING THE STRESS GREMLIN: MANAGING YOUR BEHAVIOURS 87
9. STRESS DOS AND DON'TS 107
10. SUMMING UP 113

APPENDIX: QUIZ ANSWERS 129

REFERENCES 133

Acknowledgements

Many thanks to the colleagues who have expressed their support for what I wished to achieve through this book and who have provided me with constant reminders of why this book is needed. A special thank you also goes to Maria for her invaluable advice, knowledge and unwavering support. And last, but by no means least, I would like to thank all the young people who have been courageous enough to share their stories in order to help others.

About the Author

Hi! I'm Kate, and I have worked for several years providing support for children and young people on a range of emotional issues as well as providing training and guidance for parents and professionals on emotional issues facing young people today.

The need for a book on stress management aimed directly at young people became evident through this work. This book is about empowering young people to help themselves by learning about the basics of stress and how to control it.

Some of the young people that I have worked with have kindly contributed their stories, thoughts and drawings to this book in order to help others learn how to control their stress as they have.

I hope you find this workbook fun, interesting and enjoyable as well as packed full of useful information and tools to help you manage your stress.

Happy reading and good luck with starving your Stress Gremlin!

Kate

Information for Parents and Professionals

The purpose of this workbook

Starving the Stress Gremlin provides a cognitive behavioural approach to stress management for young people. It is designed for young people to work through on their own or with the support of a parent or a professional, such as a teacher, mentor, teaching assistant or youth worker. The self-help materials included in this workbook are based on the principles of cognitive behavioural therapy (CBT), but do not constitute a session by session therapeutic programme. However, the materials contained in this workbook can be used as a resource for therapists working with young people.

Please note that the My Stress Questionnaire in Chapter 3 is a tool for young people to use to explore and get a better understanding of their own stress. However, the questionnaire is not designed to be used as a clinical diagnostic tool.

What is cognitive behavioural therapy?

CBT is an evidence-based, skills-based, structured form of psychotherapy, which emerged from Beck's Cognitive Therapy (e.g. Beck 1976) and Ellis' Rational-Emotive Therapy (e.g. Ellis 1962), as well as from the work of behaviourists such as Pavlov (e.g. Pavlov 1927) and Skinner (e.g. Skinner 1938) on classical and operant conditioning respectively. CBT looks at the relationships between our thoughts (cognition), our feelings (emotions) and our actions (behaviours). It is based on the premise that how we interpret experiences and situations has a profound effect on our behaviours and emotions.

CBT focuses on:

- the problems that the client is experiencing in the here and now
- why the problems are occurring
- what strategies the client can use in order to address the problems.

The therapeutic process achieves this by empowering the client to identify:

- negative, unhealthy and unrealistic patterns of thoughts, perspectives and beliefs
- maladaptive and unhealthy patterns of behaviour
- the links between the problems the client is facing and his or her patterns of thoughts and behaviours
- how to challenge the existing patterns of thoughts and behaviours and implement alternative thoughts and behaviours that are constructive, healthy and realistic in order to address problems, manage emotions and improve wellbeing.

Thus the underlying ethos of CBT is that by addressing unhelpful patterns of thoughts and behaviours, people can change how they feel, how they view themselves, how they interact with others and how they approach life in general – thereby moving from an unhealthy cycle of reactions to a healthy one.

CBT has been found to be effective with a wide range of emotional wellbeing and mental health issues. For example:

- anxiety (e.g. Cartwright-Hatton *et al.* 2004 and James, Soler and Weatherall 2005)
- OCD (e.g. O'Kearney *et al.* 2006)

- depression (e.g. Klein, Jacobs and Reinecke 2007).

Furthermore, guidelines published by the National Institute for Clinical Excellence (NICE) recommends the use of CBT for a number of mental health issues, including depression (NICE 2005a) and OCD (NICE 2005b).

Although there has been less research conducted on the use of CBT with children and young people than there has been with adults, evidence for its effectiveness with children and young people is continuing to grow and being reported in a number of reviews, such as Kazdin and Weisz (1998) and Rapee *et al.* (2000). Random clinical trials have shown CBT to be effective with children and young people for:

- OCD (Barrett, Healy-Farrell and March 2004)
- depression (Lewinsohn and Clarke 1999)
- Generalised Anxiety Disorder (Kendall et al. 1997; 2004)
- specific phobias (Silverman *et al.* 1999)
- social phobia (Spence, Donovan and Brechman-Toussaint 2000)
- school refusal (King *et al.* 1998).

Introduction

Do you frequently feel under too much pressure?

Do you often feel like situations are too difficult for you to cope with?

Do you feel sick, get headaches or find it hard to eat or sleep when you feel stressed?

Do you avoid doing things when you're stressed?

Do you feel like you have no control over how you react when you are stressed?

If you have answered 'Yes' to any of the above, this book is here to help you!

Starving the Stress Gremlin contains information and activities to help you understand your own stress, why it occurs and what you can do to get it under control.

The stress management techniques that you will learn as you progress through this workbook have been adapted from the basic principles of something called cognitive behavioural therapy (CBT). CBT is where a therapist helps people to deal with a wide range of emotional problems, including stress, by looking at the links between how we think (our cognition), how we feel (our physical feelings and our emotions) and how we act (our behaviours).

In the chapters and activities that follow, you will learn about how you:

- think
- feel (physically and emotionally)
- act.

And how this is key to understanding how to starve your Stress Gremlin and get your stress under control.

Because everyone's life circumstances are different, because what we find stressful can differ from person to person and because stress can affect us all in different ways, there is a lot to cover in a book on stress and how to manage it. As a result this workbook isn't short! But don't hold that against it!

The way to get the most out of *Starving the Stress Gremlin* is to work through it in its entirety. But if you want to make a quick start, please feel free to just focus on the parts that you feel are most relevant to you and your stress. And don't forget that you can always return to the other sections of the workbook in the future.

Also it's important to remember that starting to explore your stress can sometimes raise difficult issues. If it does so for you, please consider talking to someone you trust about these issues, such as a parent, relative, friend, teacher or counsellor.

1

What is Stress?

Step 1 in managing stress is to understand what stress is.

To answer the question, 'What is stress?' we first have to understand something called the *fight, flight or freeze response*.

In order to help you do this, I want us to travel back in time in a time machine...

You step out of your time machine into a world where humans live in caves and sabre-tooth tigers roam the Earth. It's one million years ago. It's the Stone Age. Not too far away from you and your time machine, there's a caveman doing his normal caveman-type things, such as searching for berries to go in a caveman-sized pie for dinner! Suddenly you realise a very vicious-looking creature is stalking the caveman, preparing to pounce. Before you can shout 'It's behind you!' in true pantomime style, the caveman turns round and comes nose to nose with a sabre-tooth tiger.

What do you think the caveman is thinking right at this point? Write an example in the thought bubble coming out of the caveman's head.

Jackson, aged 14 years, wrote 'Helppppppppppp!!!' when he did this task. Simone, aged 10 years, wrote, 'Aaarrrrggghhhhhhh!' I'm sure you will also have written something that shows the caveman realising 'Oh no! I'm in danger. I need to survive!' Because of this thought the following temporary changes will be happening inside the caveman's body.

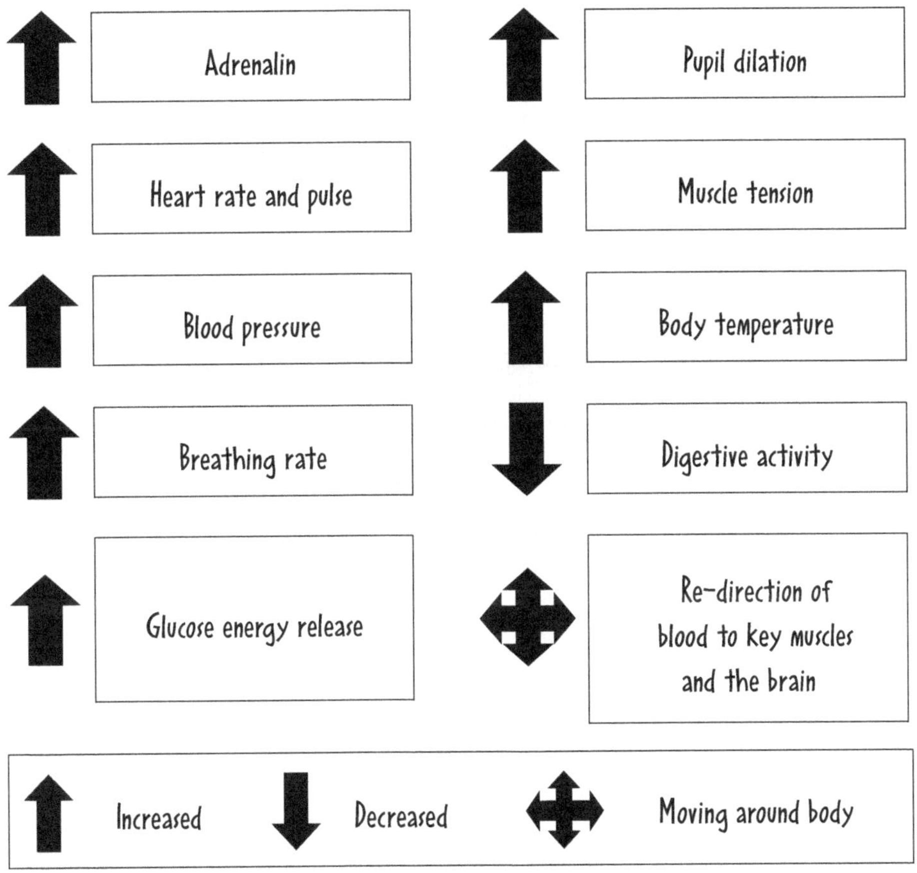

This is his body's way of preparing him to survive the encounter with the sabre-tooth tiger or any other emergency or danger he might face in his caveman life. By making all those physical changes, his body is helping him to:

RUN FASTER

SEE AND HEAR BETTER

FIGHT HARDER

JUMP HIGHER

THINK FASTER

HEAL BETTER

OK, maybe not to the extent of your average superhero, but enough to help him have a chance of surviving that head-to-head with the tiger by either:

- defending himself through fighting back (*fight*)
- defending himself through running away to safety (*flight*)
- defending himself by playing dead so the tiger leaves him alone (*freeze*).

That is the *fight, flight or freeze response* in a nutshell.

So let's now whizz forward to the present day in your time machine. Let's pretend you are a scuba diver happily diving underwater when you suddenly realise that there is a shark swimming towards you with his mouth wide open! Write in the thought bubble what you might be thinking.

Again, the thought will more than likely be one that highlights that you are in danger and you need to survive. You are facing a *real* emergency and your body will therefore trigger the very useful fight, flight or freeze response to help you deal with this emergency.

But what does this all have to do with stress?

As you will have no doubt realised, the fight, flight or freeze response is a fantastic thing, but only if it's used to help us *survive* dangerous or life-threatening *real* emergency situations as nature intended. And only if we have to face these *real* emergencies on an *infrequent* and *short-term* basis.

This fight, flight or freeze response is linked to stress and therefore has the potential to become *problematic* in two different ways:

1. When we frequently think about non-emergency situations as though they are emergencies and we think we can't cope with these situations.

2. When we are facing a number of difficult situations at one time or over a long and constant period of time that is putting pressure on us that we think we can't cope with.

Number 1: When we frequently think about non-emergency situations as though they are emergencies and we think we can't cope with these situations

This occurs when we think about non-emergency situations as worse than they actually are.

Is this a real emergency or is this an exam?

For example, thinking that your whole life's happiness and survival depend on the results you get in an exam. You might think thoughts like 'I'm going to fail' or 'The exam will be really hard and horrible and it will be the end of the world.'

Q. What is our body going to do when we start thinking in this way?

> **A.** Yes, you've guessed it – set off the fight, flight or freeze response!

The result is that we are putting our body through a *fight, flight or freeze false alarm*, where it is making physical changes to help us act in ways that we don't need in reality. Unfortunately, our bodies weren't designed to go through false alarms on a regular basis. It is supposed to be a temporary state and one that is experienced in very rare situations.

Q. What do you think the result of frequent fight, flight or freeze false alarms can be?

> **A.** Yes, you've guessed it again – STRESS!

Number 2: When we are facing a number of difficult situations at one time or over a long and constant period of time that is putting pressure on us that we think we can't cope with

We can all experience difficult situations in life. But if we are experiencing a number of difficult situations all at once and are regularly thinking negatively about our ability to cope with those situations, we are more likely to trigger off the fight, flight or freeze response and keep that response going, again leaving our body in a constant state of alarm.

Q. So what does this lead to?

A. Yes, you've guessed it once more – STRESS!

So what this tells us about stress is that it is a response to situations that put demands or pressures on us that we think we cannot cope with well enough, either because:

- We are viewing situations as worse than they are.
- We are going through a number of difficult situations at one time.

And stress brings with it a whole host of negative signs and symptoms. These can include:

COGNITIVE	PHYSICAL
Memory problems, concentration problems, obsessive thoughts, negative thoughts about yourself, unrealistic expectations of yourself, worst case scenario thoughts, 'what if?' thoughts, self-harm/suicidal thoughts, comparing self to others, mind-reading thoughts, jumping to conclusions thoughts, unrealistic thoughts about situations, thoughts that focus on negatives about situations, thoughts that things are worse than they actually are.	Sweating, headaches, hair loss, dizziness, nausea, red face, dry mouth, lump in throat, feeling hot, shortness of breath, rapid breathing, heart racing, heart palpitations, chest tightness, weight loss or gain, bowel problems, stomach ache or butterflies, skin problems and rashes, lack of appetite, shaking or tremors, jelly legs, fainting, tiredness, twitches or tics, muscle aches, pains and tension, grinding teeth, frequent urination, sleep disturbance.

BEHAVIOURAL	EMOTIONAL
Avoidance, putting off doing things, binge eating, skipping meals, making yourself sick after eating, making mistakes, acting irritably, acting aggressively, avoiding leaving the house, sleeping more or less than usual, hiding away from people, drinking, taking drugs, self-harming, skipping school/college, following rituals or routines, ignoring problems, getting into trouble, excessive exercising, taking out your feelings on others, bottling your stress up, stuttering or stammering, doing things to get people's attention, crying, smoking, committing anti-social or criminal behaviours.	Upset, agitation, feeling worthless, low mood, low in confidence, low in self-esteem, feeling under pressure, feeling overwhelmed, anger, worry, loneliness, panic, guilt, irritability, edginess, insecurity, confusion, nervousness, feeling trapped, feeling out of control, fear, dread, unhappiness, loss of motivation or pleasure or interest, hopelessness, numbness, hyper-sensitivity to things, self-criticism, self-doubt, defensiveness, suspiciousness, frustration.

Don't be disheartened if you are suffering in some of these ways. This book is here to help you learn more about stress and how to manage it! And Step 2 in this process is realising that you are not on your own in experiencing stress. So let's move on to Chapter 2 which will show you just that.

2

You're Not On Your Own

Stress in Other Young People

The research

People called researchers have asked children and young people about stress, but so far we still don't know as much about stress in children and young people as we do about stress in adults. But by asking children and young people questions face to face or through questionnaires, researchers have started to learn that:

Stress is *often* experienced by young people and is on the *increase*. For example, an NSPCC online poll of 11 to 16-year-olds found that 12 per cent of 11 to 13-year-olds and 27 per cent of 14 to 16-year-olds reported feeling stressed most of the time (NSPCC 2009).

Common sources of stress in children and young people are:

- academic worries
- family relationships
- problems at home
- friendships
- romantic relationships
- bullying
- change.

Stories from other young people

Now let's take a look at what some young people have told me about their stress:

'I believe I have to be perfect, but trying to achieve it gets me stressed. I find it hard to sleep most nights as I can't get thoughts that I'm not good enough out of my head.' (Susie, 10)

'My Mum is very sick so I have to do a lot to help my dad around the house. I don't mind doing it, but I feel stressed a lot of the time as I find it hard to fit it all in around my college work.' (Tricia, 17)

'I've been suffering with stress for a long time now and it makes me feel awful. I spend most days feeling really sick and edgy. I take it out on my friends too by snapping at them.' (Pete, 16)

'My parents expect a lot of me so I work really hard to get top marks at school and attend lots of after-school clubs. But it's too much. I often feel like I can't cope with the pressure.' (Becky, 14)

'I'm just so useless. I can't cope with anything. I just find everything stressful.' (Marlon, 11)

'My mum and dad are always arguing. I love being at school, but dread going home every evening. The atmosphere in the house is so stressful. I never know what I'm going to face when I walk through the door.' (Phil, 13)

'I moved home and school as my dad got a new job. It's been really stressful trying to make new friends and fit in. I've been trying to make myself into something I'm not to be liked, but I just can't cope with it anymore.' (Sammie, 12)

'I used to do everything I could to try and avoid going to college as I just felt so stressed whenever I was there. I have dyslexia and I find it hard to keep up in class and some people in my class bullied me about it.' (Jess, 17)

Do any of these stories sound familiar? Don't worry if they do as you can bring your stress under control just like the young people who shared their stories did!

Step 3 in this process is to learn more about your own stress. There is a questionnaire in the next chapter to help you do this.

3

My Stress

MY STRESS QUESTIONNAIRE

1. How often do you feel stressed? Tick which answer applies to you.

a) Most of the time ☐
b) Often ☐
c) Sometimes ☐
d) Rarely ☐
e) Never ☐

2. Rate the following possible sources of stress on a scale of 0 to 10, 0 being not stressful at all and 10 being very stressful.

POTENTIAL SOURCE	RATING	POTENTIAL SOURCE	RATING
School/college		Work	
Family		Friendships	
Boyfriend/girlfriend		Others' expectations of you	
Bullying		Change	
Expectations of self		Peer pressure	
The future		Your health	
Health of others		Actions of others	
Problems at home		Living environment	
Crime and safety		Attitudes of others	
Your responsibilities		The media	
World news		Exams	

3. **Think about how you tend to feel physically when you get stressed. Highlight or colour in any of the following that apply to you.**

SWEATING

HEADACHES

HAIR LOSS

DIZZINESS

NAUSEA

RED FACE

DRY MOUTH

LUMP IN THROAT

GRINDING TEETH

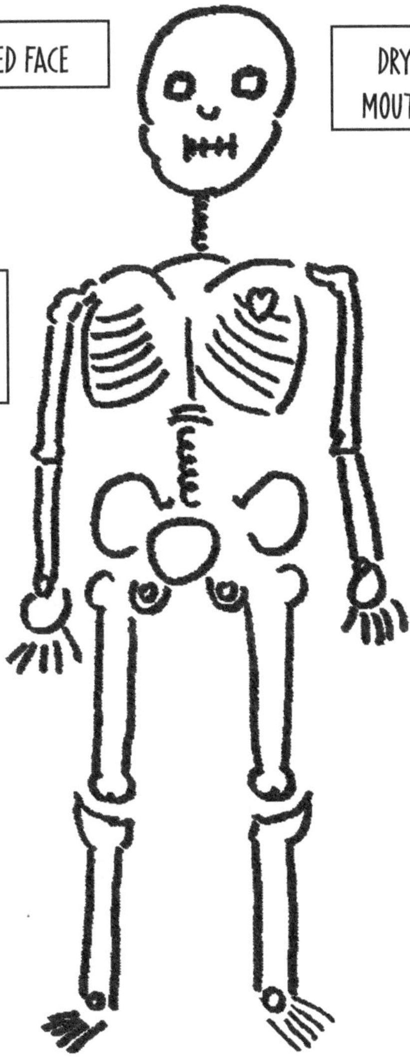

HEART RACING OR PALPITATIONS

SHORTNESS OF BREATH / RAPID BREATHING

CHEST TIGHTNESS

WEIGHT LOSS OR GAIN

STOMACH ACHE OR BUTTERFLIES

BOWEL PROBLEMS

LACK OF APPETITE

HOT

SKIN PROBLEMS

SHAKING OR TREMORS

FREQUENT URINATION

JELLY LEGS

TIREDNESS

TWITCHES OR TICS

MUSCLE PAIN, ACHE OR TENSION

FAINTING

4. Do any of the following thought patterns apply to you when you are stressed? Highlight or colour in any that apply.

'WHAT IF?' THOUGHTS	OBSESSIVE THOUGHTS	NEGATIVE THOUGHTS ABOUT YOURSELF
THOUGHTS ABOUT HARMING YOURSELF	THOUGHTS ABOUT WORST CASE SCENARIOUS	
UNREALISTIC EXPECTATIONS OF YOURSELF	THOUGHTS WHERE YOU COMPARE YOURSELF NEGATIVELY TO OTHERS	
THINKING THAT THINGS ARE WORSE THAN THEY ACTUALLY ARE	THOUGHTS WHERE YOU JUMP TO CONCLUSIONS	
UNREALISTIC THOUGHTS ABOUT SITUATIONS	FOCUSING ON NEGATIVES ABOUT SITUATIONS	
THOUGHTS WHERE YOU BLOW THINGS OUT OF PROPORTION	SELF-DOUBTING THOUGHTS	'I CAN'T' THOUGHTS

5. **Do you ever act in any of the following ways when you get stressed? Tick any that apply.**

- ☐ Avoid things
- ☐ Self-harm
- ☐ Do things to get people's attention
- ☐ Bottle your stress up inside
- ☐ Stay in bed
- ☐ Put off doing things
- ☐ Hide away from people, such as friends or family
- ☐ Deny you have a problem
- ☐ Avoid making decisions
- ☐ Binge eat
- ☐ Drink
- ☐ Take drugs
- ☐ Take out how you are feeling on others
- ☐ Act irritably towards people
- ☐ Make mistakes
- ☐ Do things that get you into trouble
- ☐ Skip school/college
- ☐ Cry
- ☐ Act aggressively
- ☐ Avoid leaving the house
- ☐ Follow rituals or routines obsessively
- ☐ Ignore problems
- ☐ Skip meals
- ☐ Smoke
- ☐ Commit crimes or anti-social behaviours
- ☐ Make yourself sick after eating

6. **Are there any other ways that you tend to act when stressed that aren't on the previous list? If so, write them down here.**

....

....

....

....

....

7. **Do you ever feel any of the following as a result of your stress? Highlight or colour in any that apply to you.**

UPSET

WORTHLESS

AGITATED

LOW IN MOOD

LOW IN CONFIDENCE

UNDER PRESSURE

OVERWHELMED

ANGRY

WORRIED

LONELY

GUILTY

INSECURE

CONFUSED

PANICKY

IRRITABLE

NERVOUS

ON EDGE

OUT OF CONTROL

AFRAID

LIKE A FAILURE

UNHAPPY

FULL OF DREAD

DEFENSIVE

SUSPICIOUS OF OTHERS

TRAPPED

8. **Does your stress have any negative effects on any of the following aspects of your life? Highlight or colour in any that apply.**

Physical health	Mental health and emotional wellbeing
Family relationships	Friendships
Performance at school/college/work/leisure activities	
Motivation to do things	Romantic relationships
Ability to concentrate	Ability to remember things

If the questionnaire revealed that you experience a lot of stress and a lot of negative stress symptoms and impacts, please don't worry. Remember that understanding more about your stress is the third step towards getting your stress under control.

So, why not have a go at another activity that can help you to understand what stress looks like for you, but this time in a more creative way. In the next Stress Box, try doing on of the following:

- Draw a picture of what your stress is like.
- Write a song/rap about your stress.
- Write a poem about your stress.
- Write a short story/play about your stress.
- Write a blog about your stress.
- Take a photo/series of photos that represent your stress.
- Take a photo/series of photos that represent your stress.
- Draw/write down ideas for a short film about your stress.
- Draw/write down ideas for a dance piece about your stress.

To inspire you, you'll find a poem that Carla, aged 16 years, wrote about her stress and some drawings created by three other young people on page 37.

STRESS BOX

Let's get creative

My Stress

My stress is a worry
In my life as a whole
It won't leave me in a hurry
And only seems to have one goal

No matter how hard I try
No matter what I say
My stress makes me cry
It's always in my way

I've lost oh so much
My stress cuts me like a knife
There's no help out there as such
I just want it gone from my life

'My Stress' by Dave, 13

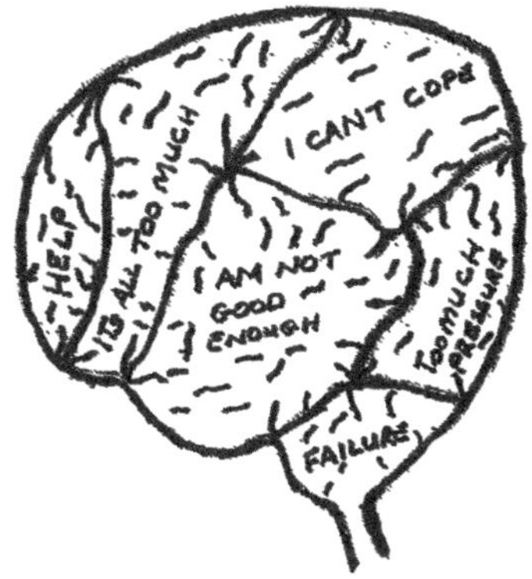

'My Stress' by Michelle, 14

So now you've learnt what your stress looks like and that you're not on your own in feeling stressed, let's look in detail at why your stress occurs. Understanding why stress occurs is Step 4 in managing stress.

4

The Stress Gremlin

How Stress Occurs

In the previous chapter you rated how stressed you felt in response to lots of possible sources of stress. Another word for these possible stress sources is *stressors*.

Stressors can be:

PLACES

PEOPLE

THINGS ABOUT YOU

SITUATIONS

ATTITUDES

ACTIONS

Another way that stressors are often categorised is:

INTERNAL STRESSORS

Come from inside us, such as physical conditions or illnesses or mental health/emotional issues.

EXTERNAL STRESSORS

Come from outside us, such as events, physical environment, external life circumstances, places, people, etc.

Here's an activity to help you understand the differences between internal and external stressors.

GIVE ME AN 'I' OR AN 'E'

Look at the list of possible stressors below and write an 'I' next to those that you think are internal stressors and an 'E' next to those that you think are external. Then highlight or circle any of them which you believe make you stressed.

STRESSOR	I or E	STRESSOR	I or E
Own illness		Being in pain	
Being put down		Change	
School/college work		Relationships	
Low self-esteem		Conflicts	
Puberty		Crime and safety	
Parental separation or divorce		Bullying	
Expectations of yourself		Exams	
Unemployment		Tiredness	
Low mood		Having a disability	
Moving home		The media	
Expectations of others		Peer pressure	

STRESSOR	I or E	STRESSOR	I or E
Noise		Death of a loved one	
Other people's attitudes		Caring responsibilities	
Your job		Extra-curricular activities	
Your sexuality		Homophobia	
Money problems		Racism	
Busy workload		Stressed parent	
Body image		Rules	

You can find the answers to this activity in the Appendix at the end of this workbook.

We are all different when it comes to what we find stressful. What one person views as stressful, another person can see as a positive challenge or as something exciting.

Why is this?

To answer that question, let's meet a troublesome creature called the Stress Gremlin!

The Stress Gremlin Model

Hungry		Feeding		Full
Stressor	→	Thoughts and beliefs	→	Stressed reaction

Stressors are often believed to *cause* stress or *make us* stressed, as though we have no control over whether we get stressed or not. This is what the Stress Gremlin wants you to think! But if this was the case, then what would be the point in trying to control our stress? We would just be puppets on a very stressed out string! And guess who'd be holding the puppet strings...your Stress Gremlin!

When you are experiencing lots of difficult situations all at once, he wants you to think that stress is inevitable. He wants you to think that there is no way to cope and that if you can't cope you are a failure. He wants you to fall apart under the pressure! He also wants you to think that other situations in life are worse than they actually are. He wants you to blow them out of proportion. He wants you to be stressed...it's what gives him a meal...it's what makes him feel full!

Thankfully, as the Stress Gremlin Model shows, stressors *don't* make us do or feel anything. They are only ever *triggers*. Think about it! If it was a situation that caused us stress, we would all feel and react in the same ways in the same situations. But we don't. As the Stress Gremlin Model shows, it is how we *think* about a situation that leads to a stressful reaction towards it. It is how we *think* about the situation that *feeds* our *Stress Gremlin*, making him bigger and bigger and fuller and fuller!

Let's look at an example scenario that highlights this.

THREE FRIENDS AND A SCIENCE EXAM

Three friends, Ashley, Charley and Sophie, aged 12, have a science exam coming up in a week's time. They are all in the same science set at school and each got a C grade in their last science exam.

Ashley

Every time Ashley sits down to revise, he thinks 'I can't do it. I'm useless! So what's the point?' As a result, he keeps putting the revision off. He does anything he can to avoid it, even cleaning the house for his mum! By the end of the week, Ashley has done very little studying and is starting to get very panicky at the thought of the exam. When he starts to panic his heart races and he finds it hard to breathe. He ends up having to spend the entire night before the exam revising.

Charley

Charley finds it difficult to remember things for exams. She believes that she will never be able to get it all to stay in her head in time for the exam and everything is feeling overwhelming. She skips breakfast and lunch every day so that she can revise non-stop. Her family make her stop for dinner, but she eats very little as she has no appetite. She ends up having a row with either her mum or dad every night about not eating. By the end of the week, Charley has fallen out with all her family, including her two sisters, and feels bad about herself. She thinks that she is going to fail the exam because she isn't a good person and she has bad dreams the night before the exam.

Sophie

Sophie knows that science isn't her best subject at school but keeps telling herself that if she revises hard, she will end up doing the best she can and that that is all that matters. She keeps reminding herself that she can do it if she tries. She sets out a revision plan, sticks to it and takes regular breaks. She spends the evening before the exam listening to music to help her relax the few butterflies she has in her stomach and sleeps well that night.

Q. Each of the three friends is facing the same situation – an exam. But do they each react in the same way? Circle your answer.

Yes No

Q. Which of the three friends seems to be the least stressed? Circle your answer.

Ashley Charley Sophie

Q. Why do you think this person ends up being less stressed about the exam than their friends?

....

....

Q. Which friends are feeding their Stress Gremlin?

....

....

Well done if you have written that:

- Each of the friends reacts in a different way to the same situation.
- Sophie appears to be less stressed than Ashley and Charley.
- It is Ashley and Charley that are feeding their Stress Gremlins.

Sophie is less stressed because she *thinks* in a different way about the exam and her ability to cope with it than Ashley and Charley do. Ashley and Charley are thinking that the situation is worse than it actually is. They are also thinking negatively about their ability to cope with it. Sophie thinks more realistically about the science exam and tries to focus on positive ways to deal with it. And because she *thinks* differently about the situation, Sophie then...

FEELS DIFFERENTLY PHYSICALLY	FEELS DIFFERENTLY EMOTIONALLY	BEHAVES DIFFERENTLY
For example: normal pre-exam butterflies.	For example: calmer, and more relaxed.	For example: positive activites to help her relax and positive actions to prepare for the exam.

Let's look at this further using something called the Stress Gremlin Cycle.

The Stress Gremlin Cycle

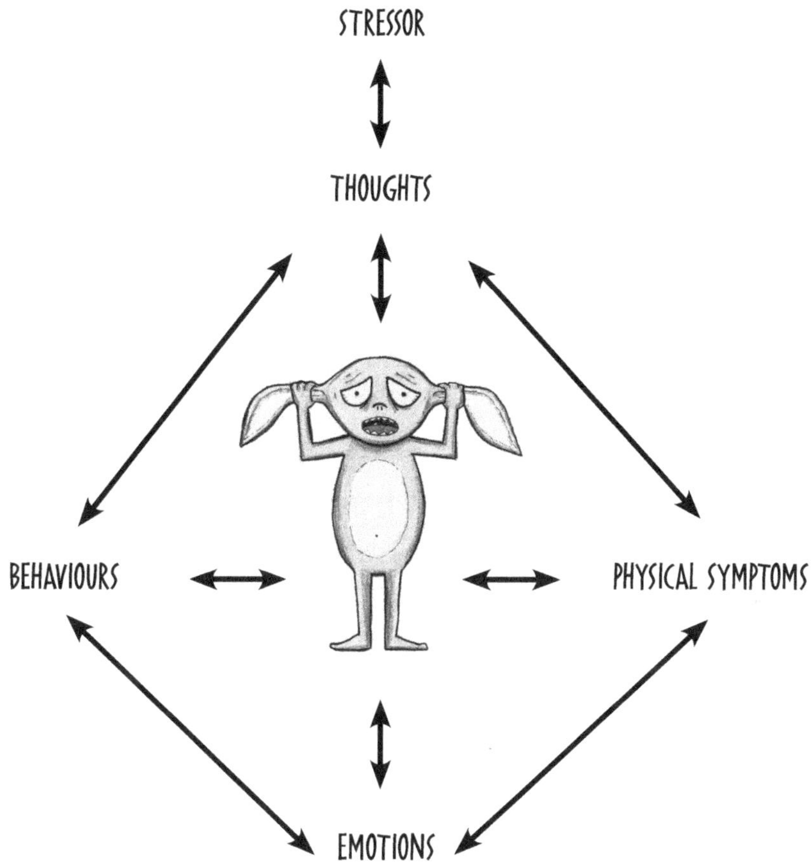

The Stress Gremlin Cycle shows the links between our thoughts, feelings and behaviours when we get stressed, and is based on a cognitive behavioural approach. It highlights how stress is maintained due to an interaction between:

- THE STRESSOR
- OUR THOUGHTS
- OUR PHYSICAL, BEHAVIOURAL AND EMOTIONAL STRESS REACTIONS.

The Stress Gremlin Cycle shows:

- If we think about a particular stressor we are facing in an overly negative or in an unrealistic way, we feed our Stress Gremlin.
- If we are facing a number of difficult situations in life and think negatively about our ability to cope with them or have unrealistic expectations about our ability to cope with them, we feed our Stress Gremlin.
- The more we feed our Stress Gremlin, the more stressed we are likely to be!
- The more we think negatively or unrealistically, the more physical symptoms of stress we are likely to experience and the more we feed our Stress Gremlins.
- The more we think negatively or unrealistically and the more we experience physical symptoms of stress, the more likely it is that our behaviours will become unconstructive and the more we feed our Stress Gremlins.
- The more unconstructive our behaviours, the more likely we are to keep focusing on the fact that we are stressed and not on how to address the situation we are facing in a constructive way and the more negative or unrealistic our thoughts will get.
- The result – we end up stuck in the middle of a vicious cycle of stress, where our Stress Gremlins get bigger and bigger and fuller and fuller and we get more and more stressed!
- We might also start to experience other negative emotions, such as anxiety or low mood, thus bringing other Gremlins along to keep our Stress Gremlins company!

So it is how we *think* about a *situation* that affects how we then feel both *emotionally* and *physically* and how we then choose to *behave*. Here's another example which highlights this.

BEN'S WORLD

Ben is nearly 15 years old and lives at home with his mum and two younger sisters. His dad moved out of the family home six months ago and his mum and dad are in the process of getting a divorce. Ben's mum has a physical condition which means her movement is very limited. She can't lift things, walk far or stand for long. Over the past six months, Ben has had to do a lot to help out around the home. Ben also goes to school five days a week to study for his exams.

The pressure of balancing home and school life is starting to take its toll on Ben. He thinks he should be able to cope with everything. He thinks that he is a failure because he is struggling. His thoughts start to revolve around him not being good enough. He also starts to blow things out of proportion, such as thinking that everything in life is going wrong. These negative thoughts then trigger a range of physical stress reactions, such as headaches.

Several months later his mum has to sell the family home because they can't afford to keep it. Ben spends a lot of time helping his mum look for somewhere else for them to live. They find a place they can afford, but it means that Ben has to make a choice to travel for one hour each way by bus every day to school or change schools in the middle of his exams. Ben decides to travel every day.

But the travelling adds to the pressure that Ben experiences as it means he now has less time to do the things he feels he must do at home. He is still thinking that the responsibility for most things in the home is his as he is now the man of the house. Ben's friends try to tell him that he needs help, but he won't listen to them. He says while anyone else would struggle with what he is going through, he should be able to cope. He tells them that he is weak and not a true 'man' if he can't look after his mum and his siblings.

Over time, his negative thoughts grow and grow and his stress levels increase.

Q. Does Ben have a lot of difficult things to deal with? If so, what are these things?

....

....

....

Q. Is Ben feeding or starving his Stress Gremlin by thinking he is weak? Circle your answer.

Feeding Starving

Q. Is Ben feeding or starving his Stress Gremlin by thinking he is a failure? Circle your answer.

Feeding Starving

It is understandable that Ben is struggling, given the amount of difficult things that he is trying to deal with. There is absolutely nothing wrong in Ben needing help. And there is nothing wrong in Ben experiencing a limited amount of stress in response to the situations he is dealing with, as experiencing *multiple stressors* at the same time can make us more susceptible to succumbing to stress. But thinking in negative ways about himself and thinking that he is weak if he can't cope with everything without help is feeding his Stress Gremlin and keeping his stress going.

Starting to believe that it is OK to ask for help and accepting that he can't do everything and that it isn't his responsibility to do everything would be ways to change his thoughts and help to bring his stress levels under control. We will look at methods like this for managing stress in more detail soon.

What you just need to remember for now is that Step 5 in managing your stress is recognising the following:

- The situation is only the trigger and **YOU** have a *choice* as to how you react to that trigger.
- **YOU** can *choose* to *think* differently.
- **YOU** can *choose* to *act* differently.

- **YOU** are in *control* of your reactions.
- **YOU** are in *control* of your Stress Gremlin.

Why not have a go at drawing your own Stress Gremlin in the Stress Box given here. Then give your Stress Gremlin a name!

STRESS BOX

My Stress Gremlin named..............................

5

Effects of Stress

When we experience stress, it can have a variety of negative impacts on us and our lives. Think about your experiences of stress and feeding your Stress Gremlin. Write in the box below how you think your stress has affected you and your life.

STRESS BOX

Effects of my stress on me

Here are some stories from other young people about how their stress has affected them.

'My stress has stopped me from achieving things that I probably could have achieved if I had just believed in myself and stressed less.' (Phillipa, 17)

'I have avoided doing lots of things due to my stress, including things that I used to enjoy doing.' (Michelle, 14)

'My stress has had an effect on my relationships with people as I get irritable with people when I get stressed, espcially my friends.' (Sandy, 12)

'I think my stress has made my health worse. I get a lot of migraines and have missed a lot of school as a result. I definitely think my migraines are due to stress.' (Chris, 15)

'The more stressed I've felt, the less confident I've felt and the more anxious I've felt.' (Melissa, 11)

'I self-harm when I get stressed. It helps at the time, but afterwards I feel guilty and stupid and useless.' (Tom, 13)

'I used to think I performed well under pressure, but these days I get too stressed and don't perform anywhere near as well. I am a runner, but since I started to get stressed, my running times have got slower.' (Mark, 16)

Our stress can also have impacts on other people around us. Again, think about times when you have got stressed. Write down what impacts you think your stress has had on other people in the box below.

STRESS BOX

Effects of my stress on others

Here are some stories from other young people about how their stress has affected other people around them.

'I have lost lots of friends due to how I react when I get stressed as I get so difficult to be around.' (Ben, 12)

'My mum and dad worry about me so much because of how stressed I get.' (Mollie, 10)

'I started drinking when I got stressed. Now I drink way too much and my friend has had to take me back to her house after evenings out so that my parents don't find out. But this is now causing rows between her and her family.' (Max, 18)

'I self-harm when I get stressed. For ages, no one knew about it. But my mum spotted a scar recently. She spoke to me about it at the time and I told her I had stopped doing it. But I can tell she doesn't believe me and that she is really worried.' (Dwayne, 16)

'When I get stressed, I also get pretty frustrated and overwhelmed. I completely lost it the other day and threw something across the room as I felt like I couldn't cope with the pressure anymore. It hit my sister. I felt so bad. I never meant to hurt her.' (Faye, 11)

'I stopped going to school for a while because of the stress it caused me. I also stopped talking to any of my friends too. When I got back to school after getting my stresses and worries under control, my best friend told me how lonely she had felt without me at school because she had been going through a tough time with some of the others in our class and I hadn't been there to support her.' (Ella, 15)

So as you can see, when we are experiencing stress frequently, intensely or over a long period of time it can have a negative impact on us and others. This can include affecting:

PHYSICAL HEALTH

FOR YOU – examples could include making you more likely to get illnesses, making current illnesses worse, making pain levels worse, experiencing digestive disorders such as ulcers, high blood pressure, heart attacks, migraines, etc.

FOR OTHERS – worrying about your stress can impact on the physical health of others around you in a variety of ways.

MENTAL AND EMOTIONAL HEALTH

FOR YOU – stress can often lead to other emotional issues, such as anxiety or low mood, as well as low self-esteem, confidence and assertiveness levels. Stress can also impact upon our happiness levels and life satisfaction in general.

FOR OTHERS – your stress can have an impact on the emotional wellbeing of others, such as your parents worrying about you a lot.

RELATIONSHIPS

FOR YOU AND OTHERS – the way you react when you get stressed can have an impact on your relationships with others, for example, if you get irritable with people when stressed.

PERFORMANCE, MOTIVATION AND FUN!!

FOR YOU – *your stress can have an impact on your motivation levels, on your interest in doing things you enjoy or have always wanted to try, your ability to perform well at things, your ability to achieve your goals and ambitions for the future and much more.*

6

Starving the Stress Gremlin

An Introduction to Stress Management

Everyone is going to experience stress at some point in their lives as life throws stressors at us all. And stress isn't too problematic if it is occasional and if we can quickly get it under control. Also, becoming stressed doesn't mean you have failed. Occasional, short-lived stress is normal. We are only human. However, this doesn't mean that we have to continually suffer high levels of stress or long-term stress. But even if you are, again this doesn't mean you have failed. It just means you need to learn some tools to help you get it under control.

Q. So how do we prevent or reduce stress?

A. By starving our Stress Gremlins!

You won't be able to starve your Gremlin overnight. It will take time. But it is possible! And you have already started this process by completing the following:

- Step 1 – Understanding what stress is.
- Step 2 – Realising you are not on your own in experiencing stress.
- Step 3 – Understanding more about your own stress.
- Step 4 – Understanding why stress occurs.
- Step 5 – Recognising that you are in control of your reactions.
- Step 6 – Understanding the effects stress can have on our lives.

All of these steps help you to start starving your Stress Gremlin. So what's next? To answer that question, think back to the Stress Gremlin Cycle again.

The Stress Gremlin Cycle

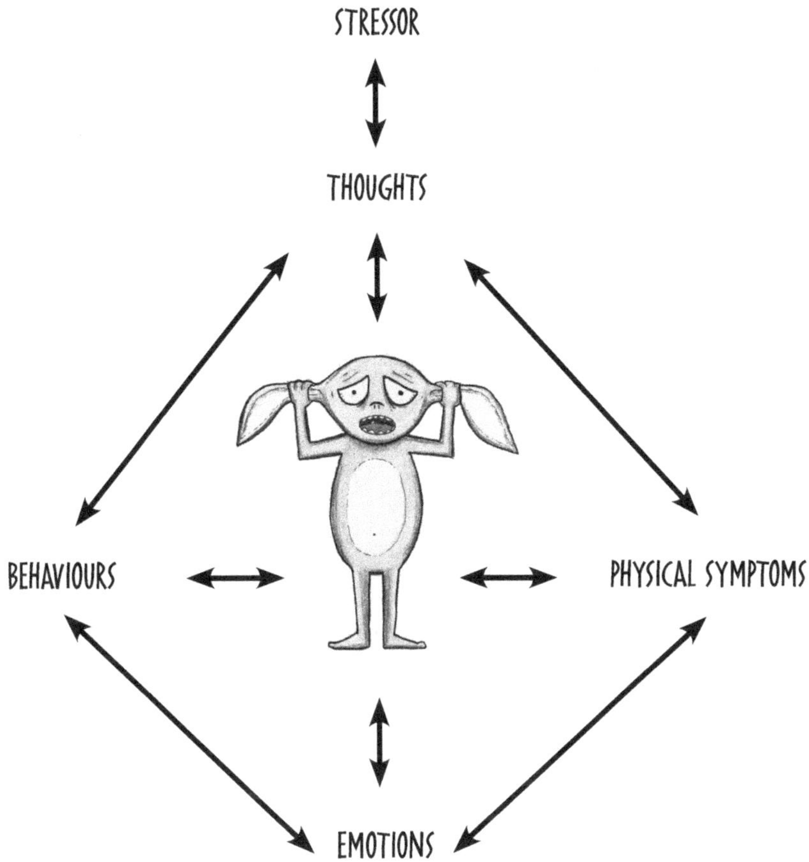

Do you remember that this cycle shows us that it is how we think and how we act that impacts on how we feel emotionally? Based on this, what do you think Steps 7 and 8 of starving your Stress Gremlin should be?

Yes, you've guessed it!

- Step 7 – Manage your thoughts.
- Step 8 – Manage your behaviours.

To help you understand what I mean by these, have a go at the following activity. Think about the last time you responded well to a stressor and then answer the questions in the Stress Box that follows.

STRESS BOX

Q. What stressor did you respond well to?

....

....

....

Q. What were you thinking in response to the stressor?

....

....

....

Q. How did you act in response to the stressor?

....

....

....

Q. What things can you learn about stress management from how you handled this situation?

....

....

....

We're going to look at a wide range of stress management strategies in the next two chapters. You may well have come up with several of them in your answers to this activity. So let's get started with Step 7 – managing your thoughts!

7

Starving the Stress Gremlin

Managing Your Thoughts

In this chapter, we will look at how you can manage your thoughts in order to starve your Stress Gremlin. The three strategies that I'm going to discuss are:

- thinking realistically
- keeping your expectations of yourself realistic
- building your self-esteem, confidence and positivity.

Don't worry if it seems like there is a lot to put into practice. All three strategies help to starve Stress Gremlins, but not all of them will necessarily be relevant to you. You just need to focus on those that are. But remember that you can also add any of the other strategies to your starving the Stress Gremlin armoury as and when you need to throughout life.

So let's start with thinking realistically.

Thinking realistically

Do you remember learning in the previous chapters that it is how you think about a situation that determines whether you experience stress? This is why *thinking realistically* starves your Stress Gremlin.

There are four steps involved in thinking realistically as the flowchart below shows.

Mindfulness → Thought-stopping → Assessment → Challenging

MINDFULNESS

Mindfulness is being aware of how you are thinking. When you find yourself starting to feel stressed, identify what you are thinking at that point in time. Many people can find this difficult to do, often because they are so distracted by the physical symptoms of stress that they are experiencing. But it is important to work hard on trying to identify your thought patterns.

Common stress-related thought patterns often involve thinking in a way that is out of proportion to the situation involved. For example:

- *Blowing things out of proportion or catastrophising* – thinking things are worse than they actually are.
- *Jumping to conclusions* – for example, making negative assumptions about a situation before knowing the facts.
- *'What if?' thinking* – worrying about what if this or what if that happens, without any evidence that they will happen.
- *Having unrealistic expectations of situations* – for example expecting a situation to go perfectly and then feeling stressed when it doesn't.
- *Focusing on negatives about situations* – for example focusing on something that is going wrong in a situation instead of how to resolve the problem.
- *Predicting worst case scenarios* – predicting the worst possible outcome.

Other stress-related thought patterns can involve thinking in an overly negative or an unrealistic way about yourself and your ability to cope with the situation. For example:

- *Putting yourself down* – focusing on your negatives and only seeing bad things about yourself.
- *Predicting failure* – continuously expecting that you will fail in some way.
- *Blaming yourself* – thinking that everything that goes wrong is your fault.
- *Having unrealistic expectations of yourself* – including your abilities to deal with a situation and your responsibilities within a situation.
- *Mind-reading* – making assumptions about what other people are thinking about you.

- *'I can't' thinking* – thoughts where you doubt yourself and your abilities.
- *Negative comparisons* – comparing yourself negatively to others.

In the world of CBT, these patterns of unhelpful thoughts are known as *thinking errors.*

To help you to be mindful of your thoughts, colour in or highlight those of the following thinking errors which tend to apply to your thought patterns when you are stressed.

STRESS BOX

WHICH THINKING ERRORS APPLY TO YOU?

PUTTING YOURSELF DOWN

BLOWING THINGS OUT OF PROPORTION

NEGATIVE COMPARISONS

BLAMING YOURSELF

UNREALISTIC EXPECTATIONS OF YOURSELF

PREDICTING FAILURE

JUMPING TO CONCLUSIONS

'WHAT IF?' THINKING

MIND-READING

'I CAN'T' THINKING

UNREALISTIC EXPECTATIONS OF SITUATIONS

FOCUSING ON NEGATIVES

PREDICTING WORSE CASE SCENARIOS

THOUGHT-STOPPING

When you notice that you are thinking a thought error type of thought, you can use one of the following techniques to help you to stop focusing on that thought for a moment:

- Say 'stop' or a similar word of your choice.
- Imagine a stop sign in your mind.

You can then take a deep breath and work on assessing and challenging your thought errors.

ASSESSMENT

To assess your thoughts, you can ask yourself questions like:

CHALLENGING

If you work out that your thoughts are unrealistic, out of proportion or overly negative in some way, you then need to challenge them based on realistic thinking. To do so, ask yourself questions such as:

So whenever you find yourself getting stressed or you are facing a difficult or challenging situation, try to think about the situation realistically based on the facts. Make sure you aren't being overly negative in some way or blowing things out of proportion and focus on what you can do to deal with the situation as best you can instead of stressing about it.

Remember situations are normally not as bad as we think they are going to be and even if our worse case scenario actually occurs, we can normally find some way to cope with it, learn from it and move on from it.

You can write your thoughts down in order to help challenge them. Some people find it easier to challenge them this way, especially in the initial stages.

The Alternative Thoughts Worksheet on the next page will help you with this and it can help you to starve your Stress Gremlin.

ALTERNATIVE THOUGHTS WORKSHEET

What is the stressor?

....

What are my thoughts in response to the stressor?

....

What are the facts about the situation?

....

Are my thoughts based on facts?

Yes No

Am I doing any of the following?

PUTTING MYSELF DOWN	BLOWING THINGS OUT OF PROPORTION	MIND-READING
BLAMING MYSELF	HAVING UNREALISTIC EXPECTATIONS	PREDICTING FAILURE
'WHAT IF?' THINKING	JUMPING TO CONCLUSIONS	NEGATIVE COMPARISONS
'I CAN'T' THINKING	PREDICTING WORSE CASE SCENARIOS	FOCUSING ON NEGATIVES

Am I stressing about something that is important or unimportant?

Important Unimportant

Are my thoughts feeding or starving my Stress Gremlin?

Feeding Starving

How can I think more realistically in order to starve my Gremlin?

....
....
....

Keeping your expectations of yourself realistic

Expectations that you might have about yourself may include believing that you need to:

- achieve a particular thing
- act in a particular way
- be a particular type of person
- look a certain way.

Let's look at an example scenario to explore the impact that our expectations can have on us and then answer the questions that follow.

PERFECTION, PERFECTION, PERFECTION!

Becky is 16 years old. She is about to take her exams. She won't be happy unless she gets top marks in every subject. She gets mad with herself if she makes a mistake in anything in life as she feels she should be perfect. She spends hours getting ready to leave the house every day as she isn't happy unless she looks perfect. She gets mad with her dad for being untidy as Becky likes everything to be neat and look nice. She is on the school netball team and wants to play perfectly every match.

Q. Do you think Becky's expectations of herself are realistic or unrealistic? Circle your answer.

Realistic Unrealistic

Q. Do you think Becky's expectations are putting too much pressure on her? Circle your answer.

Yes No

Q. Do you think Becky's expectations are feeding or starving her Stress Gremlin? Circle your answer.

Feeding Starving

What Becky's example shows us is that if your expectations of yourself are unrealistic then you are more likely to feel stressed as you are trying to achieve things that are unachievable. Thus unrealistic expectations feed your Stress Gremlin!

So in order to starve your Stress Gremlin, remind yourself that you can only ever do your best and achieve things that are realistic for you based on your abilities, strengths and current circumstances. Also remember that no one is perfect! Perfection doesn't exist!

Think about all the expectations you place on yourself. In the Stress Box given, list any expectations that you place on yourself that you now realise are unrealistic and that are feeding your Stress Gremlin.

STRESS BOX

Unrealistic expectations that I place on myself

Based on your answers to the last activity, have a go at changing your unrealistic expectations to realistic ones and write them in the Stress Box below.

STRESS BOX

Realistic expectations that I place on myself

Building your self-esteem, confidence and positivity

Our self-confidence and self-esteem involve:

- how much we like or approve of ourselves
- how worthy we think we are as a person.

Self-esteem and self-confidence develop based on the experiences and interactions we go through in our lives. This is because we start to develop certain ways of thinking about ourselves based on these experiences. For example, if a child is bullied, they might start to develop a belief that there is something wrong with them and that they aren't a likeable person.

A person with low self-esteem will often view themselves in a negative way and, as a result, are likely to have little confidence in themselves and their abilities. If you don't believe in yourself you are less likely to think that you can cope with things that come your way and are more likely to think things will go badly, for example, thinking 'I will fail.' As a result, you are more likely to experience negative emotions, such as stress. So not believing in yourself can feed your Stress Gremlin!

Let's have a look at an example scenario that highlights this and then answer the questions that follow.

THE FLOWER GIRLS

Poppy

Poppy is 13 years old and has good self-esteem. She knows there are things that she isn't good at, but doesn't expect to be good at everything. She knows what she is good at, she recognises what things in her life are good and she is proud of herself.

Lily

Lily is 13 years old. She is lacking in confidence and self-esteem. She is always thinking about the things she feels she is useless at. She is always putting herself down and focusing on what she thinks are the negatives about herself and her life. She compares herself a lot to others and believes she isn't as talented, as smart or as beautiful as her friends.

Q. Who do you think is feeding their Stress Gremlin? Circle your answer.

Poppy Lily

Q. Who do you think is starving their Stress Gremlin? Circle your answer.

Poppy Lily

A. Poppy is starving her Stress Gremlin and Lily is feeding hers.

What these flower girls show us is that in order to help starve your Stress Gremlin, you need to think more positively about yourself and your life, including:

Your positive characteristics	Your achievements and the positive things they show you about you
Your strengths	Things you are good at
The things that make you a likeable person	Times when you have successfully overcome difficulties and what they show you about you
Good things that happen to you every day	Positive things in your life
Positive goals for the future	

Use all these things to encourage and boost you at times when you feel you're struggling, when you doubt yourself and when you feel like you can't cope with something. But remember it's not about looking at yourself through rose-tinted glasses for the sake of it. It's about looking at yourself positively based on what is factual and therefore realistic. Also remember to listen more to what you know to be true about yourself based on facts and less to others' opinions of you, unless you know they are truly valid!

These will all help to starve your Stress Gremlin!

Let's try some activities to start your self-esteem building process. I asked Lily from the previous example to give her answers to each of these activities too. I have given some of these to help give you inspiration for yours.

In the Stress Box that follows, list ten positive things about yourself and write down a piece of evidence to back up each statement. To give you an example of what I mean, here are two things that Lily said about herself with accompanying evidence:

> 'I am helpful because I cook tea twice a week for my mum and sister and do the washing up most nights because my mum has a lot on her plate.'
>
> 'I am a strong person because I coped with my mum and dad's divorce even though it was a really difficult time.'

STRESS BOX

POSITIVES ABOUT ME	THE EVIDENCE

Now list at least three things you have achieved in your life so far and write down at least one positive thing that each achievement shows you about you in the Stress Box below.

STRESS BOX

My positive achievements and what they show about me

Next write down at least five strengths that you think you have that can help you to face difficult or challenging situations in life in the Stress Box below.

STRESS BOX

My strengths

Now write down at least three things you believe you are good at in the Stress Box below.

STRESS BOX

Things I'm good at

Finally, based on everything you've come up with so far, write down five positive statements about yourself in the Stress Box that follows. We call these *positive affirmations*.

To help you with this, here are Lily's positive affirmations:

'I am a good person.'

'I am likeable.'

'I try to always do the best I can.'

'I am proud of myself.'

'I believe in myself.'

STRESS BOX

My positive affirmations

It can help to place the answers to all these activities somewhere where you can look at them regularly to remind yourself of all these important things about you, especially at times when you are struggling. And remember, if you take a realistic and positive perspective on life, including how you view yourself and the expectations you have for yourself, coping with life events will be easier.

AND...you will be starving your Stress Gremlin!

OK, now let's have a look at what changes you can make to your behaviour to help you starve your Stress Gremlin – Step 8!

8

Starving the Stress Gremlin

Managing Your Behaviours

Starving your Stress Gremlin by managing your behaviours is about reducing the number of times you avoid situations and implementing more positive and constructive coping strategies. Again, I am going to list lots of different types of strategies that you can use to starve your Stress Gremlin. But again, you don't have to try and use them all. Just try those that are relevant to you. Let's start by looking at reducing avoidance.

Reducing avoidance

If you avoid things, you feed your Stress Gremlin as you don't get the opportunity to see that you can cope with the situation or that it isn't as bad as you thought it was going to be.

For example, Martin, aged ten, is feeling stressed about taking part in a school sports day as he thinks he will make a fool of himself and he decides to stay off school sick that day. By avoiding the sports day, Martin doesn't get the chance to test out whether his thoughts about making a fool of himself were true or not. He also doesn't get the chance to see that the day wasn't as bad as he thought it was going to be and that he could cope with it.

So avoidance really doesn't help in the long run because it:

- keeps the Stress Gremlin Cycle going
- feeds our Stress Gremlin
- keeps us in a state of stress!

In the next Stress Box, list any situations that you are currently avoiding in life due to your stress. Then write down what you think are the advantages and disadvantages of avoiding each situation.

STRESS BOX

SITUATIONS I'M AVOIDING	ADVANTAGES OF AVOIDING	DISADVANTAGES OF AVOIDING

Q. By avoiding situations have you been feeding or starving your Stress Gremlin?

Feeding Starving

A. Feeding your Stress Gremlin!

Implementing positive coping strategies

Putting positive and constructive coping strategies in place will help you to starve your Stress Gremlin! We're going to have a look at the following examples of positive coping strategies:

- eliminating stressors
- problem-solving
- talking
- using relaxation and distraction techniques
- having fun and enjoyment
- being organised
- being assertive
- living healthily
- using a stress diary.

ELIMINATING STRESSORS

In some cases, it may be a good idea to eliminate a stressor completely from your life if you can, or reduce the amount you experience it in some way. For example, if you have tried everything you can to cope with doing five exam subjects but are still finding the work level unmanageable, then perhaps one way forward is to eliminate one exam subject.

Think about *your* stressors...

Q. Are there any stressors you can eliminate completely from your life? If so, write them down here.

....

....

Noah, aged 14 years, gave the following answer to the same question: 'I could cut out one of my after-school activities so that I have more time to catch up on the school work that I'm behind on. This will help me to feel less stressed as I'm currently trying to fit in too much.'

Q. Are there any stressors you can limit in some way if you can't eliminate them completely? If so, write them down here.

....

....

Noah gave the following answer to this question: 'I could reduce the number of mornings and evenings that I do my paper round. This will again help me to catch up on school work as well as giving me more time to rest and have fun with my mates. Both of these things will help me to de-stress.'

However, it is important to remember that we cannot eliminate *all* stressors in life. This means we have to look at other practical ways to deal with these stressors. Therefore, let's look at some other positive coping strategies, starting with problem-solving.

PROBLEM-SOLVING

Difficult situations and problems do occur in life. However, getting stressed won't help you to resolve them. Problem-solving is a way of finding solutions to a problem in order to starve your Stress Gremlin.

When working out how to tackle a problem you need to:

- work out exactly what the problem is
- think about possible solutions to the problem
- look at the pros and cons of each solution approach
- decide which approach to take and implement it.

Let's see how you can apply the above strategies to a problem that someone else has in the following example.

CHEATING OR NOT CHEATING?

Andy is 15 years old. He is experiencing stress in response to the fact that he and his girlfriend have been having a lot of arguments recently. He now suspects she is cheating on him with one of his friends.

Q. What can Andy do to help solve the problem he is facing?

....

....

TALKING

One of your answers to the question above might have been to talk to either his girlfriend or his friend to find out if what he is stressing about is actually true. Another answer that you may have given is that he could talk to another friend or one of his parents or someone else he trusts about how he is feeling and about what he should do to handle the situation.

Talking is so important to managing stress and starving your Stress Gremlin as it can help you to:

EXPRESS HOW YOU ARE FEELING	CHALLENGE YOUR THOUGHTS	IDENTIFY WAYS TO RESOLVE PROBLEMS

Q. Which of the following people do you think you could talk to when you are stressed?

MUM	DAD	FRIEND
BROTHER/SISTER	OTHER RELATIVE	TEACHER

Q. Are there any other people that you would talk to that aren't mentioned in the previous question?

....

....

Don't forget you can talk to a professional, such as a doctor, psychologist or counsellor about things that are concerning you either face to face or through a telephone helpline. There are also many support groups available where you can go along and talk to people who are in similar circumstances to you. Your doctor, school or college may be able to put you in touch with these forms of support.

USING RELAXATION AND DISTRACTION TECHNIQUES

You can use simple relaxation techniques, such as deep breathing exercises, to help you to relax when you're feeling stressed and to starve your Stress Gremlin! Have a go at the following exercises and see what you think. It's OK if these don't feel right to you as they aren't always suitable for everybody. But give them a go and see what you think. Remember you can always try other forms of activity that are aimed at relaxation such as:

- Meditation and yoga: the word 'yoga' originates from the Sanskrit word 'Yuj', meaning to join or unite. Yoga aims to create balance and harmony in your body and mind through breathing, yoga exercise poses and meditation. Mediation involves focusing on quiet thoughts and contemplations to help you free your mind of distractions and stresses. There are different forms of both yoga and meditation.
- T'ai Chi: originating in the martial arts, T'ai Chi is now practised as a form of exercise that combines deep breathing with slow and gentle movements in order to achieve a relaxed state of mind and body.

DEEP BREATHING EXERCISE

Either sit down or lie down on your back. Focus on your breathing. Put one hand on your upper chest and one on your abdomen (just below your ribs). Gently breathe in, and as you do so, notice that your abdomen rises slowly under your hand. Slowly breathe out noticing how your abdomen falls down slowly. Repeat the process, breathing in and out with a slow, steady rhythm. You are breathing correctly if your hand on your abdomen moves up and down slowly but the hand on your chest remains still.

RELAXATION EXERCISE 1

Close your eyes and imagine yourself somewhere peaceful, happy or enjoyable. Somewhere that makes you feel relaxed and happy. Focus on that image, start to build the detail, and for a short time, imagine that you are actually there. Breathe deeply and slowly as you do.

RELAXATION EXERCISE 2

Focus on one muscle in your body at a time, and slowly tighten and then relax the muscle.

RELAXATION EXERCISE 3

Lie on your back. Breathe in deeply and slowly, imagining that the breath is coming in through the soles of your feet, travelling up through your body and exiting through your head. Breathe in again and this time imagine that the breath is coming in through your head, travelling down through your body and out through the soles of your feet. Repeat this exercise several times slowly.

VISUALISATION EXERCISES

- Imagine a calming image.
- Imagine a funny image.
- Imagine you are in a happy place.
- Imagine your stresses as visual things being discarded by you.
- Imagine yourself tackling a stressful situation and what it would look like and feel like.

Alternatively, you can use activities that you enjoy to help you relax. These same activities can also be good to help you take your mind off stressed-out thoughts that might be whirring around in your head. But in order for them to work as a distraction, the activities that you choose need to be able to fully absorb your attention.

Have a go at coming up with relaxation and distraction activities that might work for you and write them down in the following Stress Box.

STRESS BOX

Positive things I can do to relax when stressed

Positive things I can do to distract myself when stressed

Examples that you might have included in your list are:

- breathing and relaxation techniques
- exercise
- T'ai Chi
- yoga and meditation

- hot bath/shower
- listening to music
- watching TV
- spending time with friends or family
- volunteering
- extra-curricular/leisure activities
- going to the cinema
- reading.

HAVING FUN AND ENJOYMENT

It is also important to ensure that you:

- get time for you every day
- give yourself things to look forward to
- increase your positive activity levels
- try new positive challenges
- have fun!

All of these will help you to realise that life doesn't have to be all about stress! They will also give you the opportunity to feel more positive about yourself and your life and to starve your Stress Gremlin.

Q. Name one positive and enjoyable new activity you could add to your life and routine at the moment.

....

BEING ORGANISED

Learning some basic organisational skills can help you to starve your Stress Gremlin as disorganisation can be a stressor. Here's some example organisational Dos and Don'ts:

DOS

Plan things.

Prioritise – that is, work out which tasks are most important and complete those first.

Manage your time more effectively and realistically.

Set yourself realistic goals and targets.

Choose an environment to work in that isn't too distracting.

Choose a time of day to work in that suits you best.

Focus on what you have achieved.

Reward yourself for your achievements (doesn't need to involve buying yourself something, perhaps it can just involve allowing yourself an hour to do something fun you haven't had the time to do).

DON'TS

Don't get preoccupied with what you haven't achieved.

Don't put tasks off until the last minute.

Don't rush through tasks.

Don't let being organised become too obsessive as that can lead to stress too and feed your Gremlin!

Here's an activity to get you started with the organisational 'Dos'. In the Stress Box below, list all the things you have achieved today. Do this list at the end of every day for two weeks, adding in what positive things each achievement shows you about you. After a while you can do this less frequently, such as at the end of every week or once a month. But it's still important to keep it up as regularly as possible as it will remind you of just how well you are doing.

STRESS BOX

Today's achievements

Q. What do you think the things you have achieved today show you about you?

....

....

Q. What do you think your reward should be to yourself for everything you have achieved today?

....

....

BEING ASSERTIVE

As human beings, we all have certain rights.

Q. List three rights you think you have as a human.

....

....

....

You may have written three of the following or you may have picked other rights which are just as valid:

- to be treated with respect
- to say 'No!'
- to have choice
- to be listened to
- to not be physically harmed by others
- to express your opinions
- to ask for help.

When you are assertive, you recognise that your rights are equal to those of other people and you respect your own rights and the rights of others. Thus, being assertive involves:

SELF-BELIEF	RESPECTING THE RIGHTS, FEELINGS, OPINIONS AND NEEDS OF OTHERS
EXPRESSING YOUR OWN THOUGHTS, FEELINGS, OPINIONS AND NEEDS IN A CALM AND RESPECTFUL WAY	STANDING UP FOR YOUR RIGHTS IN A CALM AND RESPECTFUL WAY

These assertiveness skills are helpful to stress management in a number of ways, including helping you to:

- say 'No!' in response to unrealistic pressures or demands that can trigger stress
- solve problems that can trigger stress
- reach resolutions or compromises
- ask for help
- make complaints
- deal with conflicts that may be triggering stress
- and starve your Stress Gremlin!

LIVING HEALTHILY

Our lifestyles can also impact upon our stress levels so living healthily can help you to starve your Stress Gremlin. It is important to:

EAT A HEALTHY BALANCED DIET AND HAVE REGULAR MEALS

REDUCE THE AMOUNT OF STIMULANTS IN YOUR DIET, INCLUDING CAFFEINE AND SUGAR

DO REGULAR EXERCISE BUT NOT TOO MUCH

GET ADEQUATE SLEEP

All of the above are natural de-stressors. For example, exercise helps to use up some of the adrenalin that is released when we get stressed.

Sleep hygiene techniques can help you to improve your sleep. These include:

SLEEP ENVIRONMENT – look at what changes you may need to make to your sleep environment, such as noise levels, light levels, colours in the room, type of bed/mattress, heat levels, distractions in the room (e.g. mobile phone or TV).

PRE-BED ROUTINE – avoid anything too stimulating before bed. Do things that help you to relax instead.

SLEEP ROUTINE – getting up at approximately the same time and going to bed at approximately the same time each day can help you to sleep better.

EATING – eat at regular times as our body clock is also influenced by eating times. Also avoid stimulants as they can disturb sleep patterns.

EXERCISE – ensure you have done some physical activity in the day, but don't do aerobic exercise too close to bedtime as it stimulates the system.

IF YOU CAN'T SLEEP – get out of bed and do something relaxing and when you feel tired go back to bed and try to sleep again. Don't stress about not being able to sleep as this will only make things worse.

STRESS TIME – if you find that stressful thoughts keep you awake at night, spend a short, fixed period of time thinking about how you can tackle the things that are bothering you before you go to bed. Writing them down or talking them through with someone else can help with this.

If you are having problems with your sleep, write down what changes you think you need to make to improve your sleep in the Stress Box below.

STRESS BOX

Strategies to help improve my sleep

USING A STRESS DIARY

There is one final tool to look at that might help you when you're trying to put all the strategies into practice in order to starve your Stress Gremlin, namely a *Stress Diary*. Let's take a look at an example.

MY STRESS DIARY

Date ....

The stressor ....

What was I thinking?

....

....

How was I feeling physically?

....

....

How was I feeling emotionally?

....

....

How did I act?

....

....

What were the consequences?

....
....

Did I feed or starve my Stress Gremlin?

Feed Starve

If I fed my Stress Gremlin, what could I have done differently?

....
....

If I starved my Stress Gremlin, how did I do this and what does my success at managing my stress show me about me?

....
....
....
....
....
....

9

Stress Dos and Don'ts

Now it's time for you to think about everything we have gone through so far. Think about all the negative ways and all the positive and constructive ways of reacting to a stressor that you have learnt about. From these, I want you to come up with your own personal list of Stress Dos and Don'ts and write them in the next Stress Box. Try and come up with at least five of each! Then write down the effects that you think these Dos and Don'ts would have on you and the people around you.

Some people find it helpful to carry this list around with them in their bag or to put a copy of it up on their wall at home so that they can look at it and remind themselves of what to do at times when they are finding their stress difficult to manage.

Remember...the things that you put in your Dos column need to be things that will starve your Stress Gremlin.

STRESS BOX

DOS	DON'TS
EFFECTS	EFFECTS

Here's an example of a Dos and Don'ts list from Michael aged 12.

Dos

Think realistically about situations

Believe in myself

Talk to my friends or parents when I need help

Try and come up with ways to tackle problems that are bothering me

Go running when I feel tense

Take deep breaths if I feel myself getting stressed

Remind myself that I am good at things and that things in my life go well

Do my homework when I get it not at the last minute

Eat regular meals

Write down things that I achieve every day

Effects

Feel more confident in myself and my abilities

Have better relationships with my family

Feel calmer

Handle situations better

Be more organised

Get in less trouble at school

Be healthier

Get better marks at school

Family less stressed and upset

Get less stressed!!!

Starve my Stress Gremlin

Don'ts

Avoid things

Put off doing things

Take my stress out on other people

Blow things out of proportion

Keep thinking the worst

Worry about 'what ifs?'

Keep telling myself I'm rubbish

Shout at people

Miss lessons at school

Eat too much rubbish

Effects

Lots of stress

Never get to see that I can do better than I think I can

Feel rubbish about myself

Low confidence

Fall out with family

Family get upset

Get in trouble at school

Don't do as well as I can at school

Feel bad physically

Feel guilty and annoyed with myself

Hate self

Put too much weight on

Get upset and worry a lot

Feed my Stress Gremlin

Now you have learnt about stress management techniques and have come up with your own list of stress Dos and Don'ts, try the following activity. In the next Stress Box, write down your list of stressors again and then write down what you can do in response to each stressor.

STRESS BOX

MY STRESSORS	HOW I CAN RESPOND TO MY STRESSORS

10

Summing Up

We have now gone through all the methods you may need to starve your Stress Gremlin and get your stress under control. It's now down to you to put them into practice. But don't forget you may not need them all. Just work on implementing those that are relevant to you and your stress.

REMEMBER...

Only YOU can change how you react!

YOU'RE the one in control of your stress reactions!

YOU have all the power to starve your Stress Gremlin!

Let's have a quick recap before we finish.

Write down five things that you have learnt about your stress and how to control it in the Stress Box below.

STRESS BOX
What I have learnt

Now try applying your new knowledge to the last time you felt stressed. Answer the questions in the Stress Box below and be proud of just how much you have learnt about your stress and how to starve your Stress Gremlin!

STRESS BOX

Think about a recent time when you felt stressed.

Q. What happened?

....

....

Q. How did you think about the situation?

....

....

Q. How did you feel?

....

....

Q. How did you act?

....

....

Q. What effects did it have on you and other people?

....

....

Q. How could you have handled it differently?

....

....

Let's also check what you have learnt by taking a Stress Quiz!

THE STRESS QUIZ!

1. Name three physical signs of stress.

1. ....

2. ....

3. ....

2. Fight, Flight .... Response. What is the missing word?

a) Melt ☐

b) Freeze ☐

c) Refrigerate ☐

3. Name three types of stress thinking errors.

1. ....

2. ....

3. ....

4. What is a thing or situation that triggers your stress called?

a) An annoyer ☐

b) A stressor ☐

c) A frustrator ☐

5. Which of the following can affect your ability to control your stress?

a) Past experiences ☐

b) Lots of current stressors ☐

c) Your core beliefs about yourself and the world ☐

d) All of the above ☐

6. Name three unconstructive ways to behave when you get stressed.

1. ....

2. ....

3. ....

7. What do you need to do to your Stress Gremlin?

a) Feed it ☐

b) Starve it ☐

8. Name three ways to starve your Stress Gremlin.

1. ....

2. ....

3. ....

9. Name the five parts of the Stress Gremlin Cycle.

1. ....

2. ....

3. ....

4. ....

5. ....

10. Write down one question you should ask yourself when you begin to get stressed.

....

11. Name two aspects of your life your stress can affect.

1. ....

2. ....

12. Who is in control of your stress?

a) A place ☐

b) Another person ☐

c) An event ☐

d) You ☐

Turn to the Appendix to see how you've got on!

Well done! I'm sure you did great!

Now have a go at a more creative way of reinforcing what you have learnt with the following activity.

YOUR VOICE! TEACHING OTHER YOUNG PEOPLE ABOUT STRESS

If you wanted to spread the word far and wide to other young people about stress and how to manage it, what would you do?

Pick whether you would:

- design a webpage for young people to access
- design a poster campaign for schools and colleges
- design scenes for a TV advert
- give a talk at schools and colleges
- deliver a play at school and colleges.

Then, in the space below, jot down ideas on the kinds of things you would include in whichever type of campaign method you would use. And if you want to have a go at completing your campaign advert, website, poster, etc., on some separate paper or on a computer go ahead. Just think, maybe your school or college might want to use it!

Now let's check on how your stress has changed during the course of reading this book by re-taking the My Stress Questionnaire. You will notice that there are now three extra questions at the end! Have a go at answering the questions to see how well you've been starving your Stress Gremlin.

MY STRESS QUESTIONNAIRE

1. How often do you feel stressed? Tick which answer applies to you.

a) Most of the time ☐

b) Often ☐

c) Sometimes ☐

d) Rarely ☐

e) Never ☐

2. **Rate the following possible sources of stress on a scale of 0 to 10. 0 being not stressful at all and 10 being very stressful.**

POTENTIAL SOURCE	RATING	POTENTIAL SOURCE	RATING
School/college		Work	
Family		Friendships	
Boyfriend/girlfriend		Others' expectations of you	
Bullying		Change	
Expectations of self		Peer pressure	
The future		Your health	
Health of others		Actions of others	
Problems at home		Living environment	
Crime and safety		Attitudes of others	
Your responsibilities		The media	
World news		Exams	

3. **Think about how you tend to feel physically when you get stressed. Highlight or colour in any of the following that apply to you.**

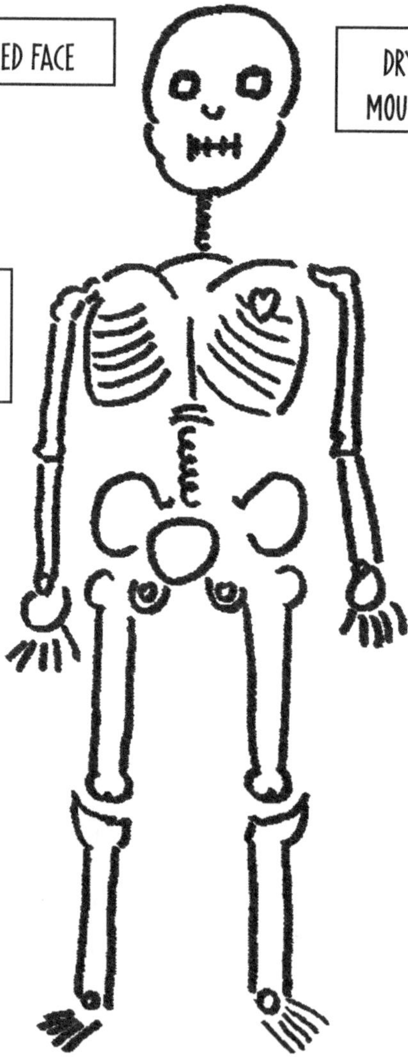

4. **Do any of the following thought patterns apply to you when you are stressed? Highlight or colour in any that apply.**

- 'WHAT IF?' THOUGHTS
- OBSESSIIVE THOUGHTS
- NEGATIVE THOUGHTS ABOUT YOURSELF
- THOUGHTS ABOUT HARMING YOURSELF
- THOUGHTS ABOUT WORST CASE SCENARIOUS
- UNREALISTIC EXPECTATIONS OF YOURSELF
- THOUGHTS WHERE YOU COMPARE YOURSELF NEGATIVELY TO OTHERS
- THINKING THAT THINGS ARE WORSE THAN THEY ACTUALLY ARE
- THOUGHTS WHERE YOU JUMP TO CONCLUSIONS
- UNREALISTIC THOUGHTS ABOUT SITUATIONS
- FOCUSING ON NEGATIVES ABOUT SITUATIONS
- THOUGHTS WHERE YOU BLOW THINGS OUT OF PROPORTION
- SELF-DOUBTING THOUGHTS
- 'I CAN'T' THOUGHTS

5. Do you ever act in any of the following ways when you get stressed? Tick any that apply.

☐ Avoid things

☐ Self-harm

☐ Do things to get people's attention

☐ Bottle your stress up inside

☐ Stay in bed

☐ Put off doing things

☐ Hide away from people, such as friends or family

☐ Deny you have a problem

☐ Avoid making decisions

☐ Binge eat

☐ Drink

☐ Take drugs

☐ Take out how you are feeling on others

☐ Act irritably towards people

☐ Make mistakes

☐ Do things that get you into trouble

☐ Skip school/college

☐ Cry

☐ Act aggressively

☐ Avoid leaving the house

☐ Follow rituals or routines obsessively

☐ Ignore problems

☐ Skip meals

☐ Smoke

☐ Commit crimes or anti-social behaviours

☐ Make yourself sick after eating

6. Are there any other ways that you tend to act when stressed that aren't on the previous list? If so, write them down here.

....

....

....

....

....

....

7. **Do you ever feel any of the following as a result of your stress? Highlight or colour in any that apply to you.**

UPSET · WORTHLESS · AGITATED · LOW IN MOOD

LOW IN CONFIDENCE · UNDER PRESSURE · OVERWHELMED

ANGRY · WORRIED · LONELY · GUILTY

INSECURE · CONFUSED · PANICKY · IRRITABLE

NERVOUS · ON EDGE · OUT OF CONTROL

AFRAID · LIKE A FAILURE · UNHAPPY · FULL OF DREAD

DEFENSIVE · SUSPICIOUS OF OTHERS · TRAPPED

8. **Does your stress have any negative effects on any of the following aspects of your life? Highlight or colour in any that apply.**

Physical health	Mental health and emotional wellbeing
Family relationships	Friendships
Performance at school/college/work/leisure activities	
Motivation to do things	Romantic relationships
Ability to concentrate	Ability to remember things

9. Have you seen any changes in your stress since you completed the My Stress Questionnaire at the start of the book? Circle your answer.

a) Yes b) No

10. If you have seen changes in your stress, what are these changes?

....

....

....

....

11. What goals would you like to set yourself so that you can continue to improve your ability to manage your stress?

....

....

....

....

I hope that you have seen your stress levels start to reduce and the way you are responding to potential stressors starting to change too. As you continue to put everything you have learnt from this book into practice, occasionally ask yourself the questions from the My Stress Questionnaire to monitor how far you've progressed and how well you're starving your Stress Gremlin! Also keep re-visiting the activities in the book to help you along the way.

But please be patient with yourself when putting all you've learnt into practice. You won't change everything overnight and remember no one gets it right all the time. No one is perfect!

And remember...

Sometimes life can be difficult.

But *you* are in control of how you react when stressors come along.

You are in control of your stress and you can starve your Stress Gremlin!

Just believe in *you*!

Good luck!

Appendix: Quiz Answers

GIVE ME AN 'I' OR AN 'E'

STRESSOR	I or E	STRESSOR	I or E
Own illness	I	Being in pain	I
Being put down	E	Change	E
School/college work	E	Relationships	E
Low self-esteem	I	Conflicts	E
Puberty	I	Crime and safety	E
Parental separation or divorce	E	Bullying	E
Expectations of yourself	I	Exams	E
Unemployment	E	Tiredness	I
Depression	I	Having a disability	I

STRESSOR	I or E	STRESSOR	I or E
Moving home	E	The media	E
Expectations of others	E	Peer pressure	E
Noise	E	Death of a loved one	E
Other people's attitudes	E	Caring responsibilities	E
Your job	E	Extra-curricular activities	E
Your sexuality	I	Homophobia	E
Money problems	E	Racism	E
Busy workload	E	Stressed parent	E
Body image	I	Rules	E

THE STRESS QUIZ

1. You may have included any physical signs of stress from the list on page 23, such as loss of appetite, tiredness and grinding teeth.
2. (b) Freeze.
3. You may have included any thought errors from the box on page 68, such as predicting failure, predicting worst case scenarios and negative comparisons.
4. (b) A stressor.
5. (d) All of the above.
6. You may have included some of the behaviours from the list on page 24, such as bottling up your stress, putting off doing things and binge eating.
7. (b) Starve it.
8. You may have included any of the eight steps towards managing your stress given on pages 62–63, such as understanding how stress occurs. You may have also included any of the managing thoughts and managing behaviours discussed in Chapters 7 and 8, such as thinking realistically and being assertive.
9. Trigger, thoughts, physical symptoms, emotions and behaviours.
10. You may have included any of the questions in the thought bubbles on pages 69–70, such as 'Are my thoughts based on facts?'
11. You may have included any of the effects from those given on pages 58–59, such as physical health and relationships.
12. (d) You.

References

Barrett, P., Healy-Farrell, L. and March, J.S. (2004) 'Cognitive-behavioural family treatment of childhood obsessive compulsive disorder: a controlled trial.' *Journal of the American Academy of Child and Adolescent Psychiatry 43*, 1, 46–62.

Beck, A. T. (1976) *Cognitive Therapy and Emotional Disorders*. New York: International Universities Press.

Cartwright-Hatton, S., Roberts, C., Chitsabesan, P., *et al.* (2004) 'Systematic review of the efficacy of cognitive behaviour therapies for childhood and adolescent anxiety disorders.' *British Journal of Clinical Psychology 43*, 421–36.

Ellis, A. (1962) Reason and Emotion in Psychotherapy. New York: Lyle-Stuart.

James, A.A.C.J., Soler, A. and Weatherall, R.R.W. (2005) 'Cognitive behavioural therapy for anxiety disorders in children and adolescents.' *Cochrane Database of Systematic Reviews* 2005, Issue 4. Art. No.: CD004690. DOI: 10.1002/14651858.CD004690.pub2. Published online January 2009.

Kazdin, A.E. and Weisz, J.R. (1998) 'Identifying and developing empirically supported child and adolescent treatments.' *Journal of Consulting and Clinical Psychology 66*, 19–36.

Kendall, P.C., Flannery-Schroeder, E., Panichelli-Mindel, S.M., Sotham-Gerow, M., Henin, A. and Warman, M. (1997) 'Therapy with youths with anxiety disorders: a second randomized clinical trial.' *Journal of Consulting and Clinical Psychology 18*, 255–70.

Kendall, P.C., Safford, S., Flannery-Schroeder, E. and Webb, A. (2004) 'Child anxiety treatment: Outcomes in adolescence and impact on substance abuse and depression at 7.4 year follow-up.' *Journal of Consulting and Clinical Psychology 72*, 276–287.

King, N.J., Molloy, G.N., Heyme, D., Murphy, G.C. and Ollendick, T. (1998) 'Emotive imagery treatment for childhood phobias: a credible and empirically validated intervention?' *Behavioural and Cognitive Psychotherapy 26*, 103–13.

Klein, J.B., Jacobs, R.H. and Reinecke, M.A. (2007) 'A meta-analysis of CBT in adolescents with depression.' *Journal of the American Academy of Child and Adolescent Psychiatry 46*, 1403–1413.

Lewinsohn, P.M. and Clarke, G.N. (1999) 'Psychosocial treatments for adolescent depression.' *Clinical Psychology Review 19*, 329–42.

National Institute for Clinical Excellence (NICE) (2005) 'Depression in Children and Young People. Identification and Management in Primary, Community and Secondary Care.' *Clinical Guideline 28*. Available at www.nice.org.uk/guidance/CG28, accessed on 2 January 2013.

National Institute for Clinical Excellence (NICE) (2005) 'Obsessive Compulsive Disorder: core interventions in the treatment of obsessive compulsive disorder and body dysmorphic disorder.' *Clinical Guideline 31*. Available at www.nice.org.uk/nicemedia/pdf/CG031niceguideline.pdf, accessed on 2 January 2013.

NSPCC (2009) 'One in three children feel some distress most of the time.' NSPCC Press Release, 19 October. Available at www.nspcc.org.uk/news-and-views/media-centre/press-releases/2009/09-10-19-one-in-three-children-feel-some-distress/09-10-19_one_in_three_children_feel_some_distress_most_of_the_time_wdn75033.html. Accessed 20 September 2012.

O'Kearney, R.T., Anstey, K., von Sanden, C. and Hunt, A. (2006) 'Behavioural and cognitive behavioural therapy for obsessive compulsive disorder in children and adolescents.' *Cochrane Database of Systematic Reviews* 2006, Issue 4. Art. No.: CD004856. DOI: 10.1002/14651858.CD004856.pub2. Published online January 2010.

Pavlov, I. P. (1927) *Conditioned Reflexes: An Investigation of the Physiological Activity of the Cerebral Cortex*. Translated and edited by G. V. Anrep. London: Oxford University Press.

Rapee, R.M., Wignall, A., Hudson, J.L. and Schniering, C.A. (2000) *Treating Anxious Children and Adolescents: An Evidence-Based Approach*. Oakland, CA: New Harbinger Publications.

Silverman, W.K., Kurtines, W.M., Ginsburg, G.S., Weems, C.F., Rabian, B. and Setafini, L.T. (1999) 'Contingency management, self-control and education support in the treatment of childhood phobic disorders: a randomized clinical trial.' *Journal of Consulting and Clinical Psychology 67*, 675–87.

Skinner, B. F. (1938) *The Behavior of Organisms*. New York: Appleton-Century-Crofts.

Spence, S., Donovan, C. and Brechman-Toussaint, M. (2000) 'The treatment of childhood social phobia: the effectiveness of a social skills training-based cognitive behavioural intervention with and without parental involvement.' *Journal of Child Psychology and Psychiatry 41*, 713–26.

This is to certify that

....

has successfully completed the
Starving the Stress Gremlin
workbook and can expertly

**STARVE THEIR
STRESS GREMLIN!**